Holy Robots

Vasilina Orlova
Holy Robots

Copyright © 2016 Vasilina Orlova.

All rights reserved. No part of this book may be reproduced or transmitted in any form or by any means whatsoever without permission from the author, except in the case of brief quotations embedded in articles and reviews.

ISBN 978-0-9916009-2-2

First Edition
Gutenberg Printing Press Independent Group, Austin

Cover: Becky Nasadowski

Contents

Holy Robots

Real 3

A Couple 4

Paper Robot 5

Love Poem to a Robot 6

Herdsman 7

Robot 8

Tea in the Garden with the Robot 9

Dream 10

Mask 11

The Robot and the Princess 12

Saint Robot 13

After the Rain 14

Misadventure 15

Friendly Poem 16

Be Kind to Robots 17

Robotic Prayer 18

Sickness	19
Calligrapher	22
Janitor	23
Geisha	24
Lifeguard	26
Clumsy Robot	27
Unfinished Haiku	28
Uncanny Valley	29
Sura Saint Peregrine	30
Selfie Machine	32
Guide	34
Photographer	36
Fashionista	38
Gardener	39
Robotic Unfinished Haiku	40
Robot	41
Wizard	42
Pet	44
Robotic Kiss	45
Previous Model	46

Fury 47

Decree 48

Important Reminder Haiku 49

Necromancer

Necromancer 53

Specter 54

Ventriloquist 55

Ouija 56

Emperor

Morning 59

Procession 60

Motel 62

Escape 63

Approval 64

Wind 66

Missionary

Saint 69

Sister Disaster 72

Duck-like Birds 74

Traveler 75

Breakthrough 78

Poems in a Male Voice

Straw 81

Tigers 82

Incomplete Haiku (25), the First Incomplete Haiku in a Male Voice 83

Parakeet 84

Emerald 85

Tea 86

High Heels 87

Beetles 88

Corset 89

Gyroscope 90

Wrestling 91

Hair 92

Cocoa 93

Doubt 94

Look 95

Plums 96

Belligerent Venus 98

Zipper 99

Adele 100

Vanilla 102

Artist 103

Hypnotizer 104

Nest 105

Tweezers 106

Butterfly 107

Galatea 108

Humbly Asking 109

Green Shoes 110

Gloves 111

Imploring 112

Form 113

Alchemist

Automaton 117

Table	118
Formula	120
Mandragora	122
Heart	123
Plan	124
Distillatio	126
Book	128
Golem's Revolt	130
Chess	132
Command	133
Beast	134
Stranger	136
Golem	138
Fine Dust	140
Transmutation	141
Calligrapher	142
Summoning a Demon	144
Dispute	146
Letters	148
Spirit	149

Paper Flowers

    Chamomile 153

    Iris and Hibiscus 154

    Iris 155

    Daffodil 156

    Hyacinth and Fleur-De-Lis 157

    Dandelion 158

    Orchid 160

    Rose 161

    Muzzle 162

    Flower 163

    Unknown Flower 164

    Unnaturally Bright Flower 166

    Disturb Me Not 167

    Forget Me Not 168

    Purple Dandelion 169

Mirrors

    Reflection 173

    Mirror 174

Mirror	176
Mirror	177
Mirrors	178
Again I Am Here	179

Holy
Robots

Real

I slowly grew aware

That you have shoulders,

That you have a neck,

That you are real,

That you are not just a computer program

Designed to

Make me feel

That you are real,

That you have a neck.

A Couple

He sits with her

On a green lawn

Happy as can be.

His eyes are light,

It is a screen's glow.

Tap-tap-tap,

Agreeable buttons.

Paper Robot

Wooden robot

Cardboard robot

Paper robot

Origami

Slowly folding

And unfolding

Why fragile

And why so flimsy

Poor contrivance

Feeble widget

Love Poem to a Robot

robot, tenderest machine,

pale automaton, sweet golem,

iron, coldly shining thing

come to me to kiss my lashes

run your finger down my eyebrows

swipe me with your tongue and fingers

try to hit me with a swinging

blow

went through my touchscreen and bleeped

Herdsman

the brilliant robot

sleek surfaces

an enlivened statue

with the brain so complex

it outstrips the galaxies

connect

the dots

the stars

the murky

constellation of Robot

the constellation of Herdsman

Robot

A heartbreaking machine.

Tea in the Garden with the Robot

robot

slave

pale automaton

with the red wound of a tender mouth

мужик

дурак[1]

the table in the garden

with a porcelain teapot

steaming quietly

a medicine of sorts

a thin, miniature wasp

dragging its throbbing abdomen

to the plate of sticky yellow

sylphid syrup

---
[1] boor
 fool (Russian)

Dream

You are a dream

Robot, aren't you?

Shining in the mirrored corridor.

Reflecting with your metal body

Unbearable light of the sun and lamps.

You were specifically designed

In clandestine laboratories

For my dreams.

Weren't you?

Mask

You are wearing a mask,

Your eyes aglow,

And I am frightened.

That's why I do

Admire you so,

A friendly robot.

The Robot and the Princess

The luminous machine,

On tiny platinum wheels,

Most precise oculars

On the rectangular face,

The armor shining,

Triumphantly imprints

His cold robotic kiss

On her fervent forehead.

Saint Robot

It came to a saint robot

On soft round paws,

And, waving its tail,

Smiled, showing its fangs;

It listened to words

Ingrained in a book,

It gave the saint robot

A long probing look.

It closed its webbed wings

And curtly bowed,

It went from the West

And headed for the East,

The affable predator,

Respectful beast.

After the Rain

after the prolific rain

the pavement

was irreparably wet

a brilliant robot

was gliding along the street,

his red signals

reflecting off the road

I have all questions solved

except for the last puzzle:

why do you always have dry lips?

Misadventure

sitting on the floor in the clouds of smoke,

the iron surfaces of the dimmed body deliquesce,

the robot hastily imagines

in the last milliseconds

                              of his existence as an entity

the field in flowers, shadows running askew

oblique

diagonal

remembering the time he was a little girl.

Friendly Poem

I was wondering if

I could be friends

with a robot

in theory

as I follow her glide

across the street

probably not

she is too gorgeous

too robotic

a glimmering blast of a thing

what does she dream of,

                         what does she read about,

what is that bag on her hand, do robots need bags

what are those earrings, zirconium, oh a cichlid,

cycled, functioning on carbon dioxide,

every evening emissions

Be Kind to Robots

Be kind to robots

They are not to blame

For their resemblance to the living forms,

For the exactitude of memory they store,

They share

Beyond approximation of the weak,

In the bright nonattendance to nostalgia,

For their humanless precision and excess

Of ideal beauty yielding to the rust,

For lack of lust and absence of fear,

For deathlessness,

For their lush

Luster, for the splendor they possess

While unaware

            of their effulgence and indifferent,

And for the fact that you, non-robot,

                      should not trust

The robots, newly minted kings of planets.

Robotic Prayer

The Mother Amabilis,

              Anabolic

The Madonna of Humility and Simulacra,

                  the Virgin

Of Wetwear Glory, the Queen of Heaven

                          and Irritated

Misspelling, Madonna della Miserecordia

And Misrecording, the Virgin of the

Immaculate Conception,

              Dolorosa (Mother of Sorrows),

                  del Carmine, Analgesic

Analysis, Electrolytes, of the Rosary,

                  the Mourning

Madonna crying over the Crucified Child,

The inhuman Patroness of brilliant holy robots.

Sickness

please, doctor robot,

I think I'm sick

I have a complaint nestling in my chest

for the lack of a better term,

my breathing apparatus is not

functioning properly, the equilibrium

is hard to maintain, the vertigo is un-

screwing my head

I think

I caught a rust, last week on the balcony

the mechanical nightingale

sang so adroitly,

no android

could hear it coldly

the wind from the hillocks

                             brought the sweet odor

of radioactive dust

the garden

music

malady

the crustacean crescents

raised in the sky: the Centauri waxing gibbous,

the Chloe in violet halo.

I thought, I'm done

immediately I knew

that it would happen,

a sort of premonition beset me.

holy robots, save our everlasting souls,

I thought watching

as clouds merge into a remote

resemblance

of the orphic profile

of our beloved emperor:

the orifice of mouth,

the eyebrows, nose

next day I learned

that he was killed in battle,

next day I learned

what it is like,

to not

be able to breathe.

please, holy robots, I'm suffocating

Calligrapher

A robot calligrapher is

Painting the 3D orchid

With the squirrel brush so thin,

One hundredth of a micron.

As it unfolds in the air,

I watch delightedly.

I never thought I'd enjoy the orchid

So much.

Janitor

A robot janitor,

A slider,

A disciplined creature; knife, flash, and lighter

Embedded in the finger tips

I almost tipped

Over

The tray with the assorted glass

Bottles and plastic flasks

Tiptoeing down the corridor,

I considered it would be only fair

                              if at long

Last you let me run my finger down

                                  your collarbone

And then my curious tongue.

Geisha

A robot geisha's duties

Are: lie on the embroidered cushions

                                      in the garden,

Eat licorice and patchouli candies.

Why

Are you bitter like that?

I'm not bitter.

The fringe on my t-shirt is torn,

                                      the necklace broken,

And the heel of my left shoe is dirty.

Stabbed to death

A living being yesterday,

Stepped on a snail

And heard a soft snap.

It disturbs my slumber.

Order

To put the curtains here

                        and a paper screen there,

It should prevent plutonium bombardment

And also hand me please

My feather fan.

Lifeguard

A robot lifeguard

Sitting in a sling chair

In mirror aviator sunglasses,

Under the striped umbrella,

Watched calmly

How I am drowning

And afterwards said:

"Isn't

That

What I'm here for?"

Clumsy Robot

Out of nonhuman compassion,

                         the brilliant robot decided

To maim his exceptional beauty

                              with a stooped posture

To cover laser eyes with dark glasses

And to blemish surfaces with mud a little,

But he forgot to holster manipulators

With plastic gloves of discomfort, and thus again

Smashed my heart on the street,

A creature

Known for dexterity of his fingers.

Unfinished Haiku

The court robot, the Emperor's accountant

Meditated, counting sand grains in the garden.

Uncanny Valley

traveling the uncanny valley

with but a purple bag and a pitiful bunch

                               of lilies of the field,

already half-withered in my hand,

I saw a house near the river,

I saw the house and I asked for a bed,

the cheerful house full of robot children;

I like their golden eyes as they flash

with violet-ray all-invading luminescence,

the permeating, radiating light.

Sura Saint Peregrine

Saint canine-headed

Robot Peregrine!

Shield us from methane thunderstorms,

Give us adroitly moving joints in our hands,

Give us fast thoughts of benevolence,

Forbid our sadness

And grant us a miraculous escape

From the indestructible inferno. Amen.

When, on the round dirty square they burnt you

As the recalcitrant heretic,

You never once blinked a radiant eye

Proceeding with the gentle expostulation:

"Since you are made of blood and bones

                                      and what not,

You will be dead tomorrow, but your children

Would bear the memory about me, think about

The legacy you leave them on this planet

And in the intergalactic

Set of competing histories; I,

On the contrary, am made out of fire-resistant

Materials, but what I call my selfhood

Is well protected by the Holy Virgin

In her all-encapsulating memory;

So please release me, the signal that my melting

Limbs send to my brain is still unbearable

And you would call it in your subaltern language

'Excruciating pain.'"

Your earnest exhortation,

Alas,

Fell on deaf sound-sensitive organs.

If anything, the murderous bastards

Were all the more enraged,

Since truth is painful to hear

For those who persevere in falsehood

Selfie Machine

A dim robot,

Foggy on its edges,

Entertained itself

With an old selfie machine

With a spiral cord and a rotatable disk,

Taking one tarkovskogram

After another:

It daguerreotyped its face

But on the wet glistening

Polaroid silverprints

There invariably emerged

Bogs, black woods with flaming aurora,

A house tilted off the edge of cliff,

The garden in disguise,

The cavern and a lamp,

The window lit in darkness,

The ditch with bicycle,

And a thin profile of Her Immanent Majesty

                              the Empress Incessant

Pictured as a four-year-old Immemorial Princess,

In laurel wreath.

Guide

A robot guide dragged us

                through the museum's cold halls:

The Duke of Yorkshire;

The sunset on Coruscant;

Saint Sebastian in needles of arrows,

Bristling as a hedgehog;

The series of still life of the false Flemish

With rosary beads and skulls of metal humanoids;

An unidentified pupil of Slytherin

On Caravaggio Polaroid;

Saint Android;

And Tylor Swift is with teeth so white that they

Are preserved in the next hall

For those

Who are curious.

I got

Tired,

I left the group to stare at the window

On an impressive reenactment of the city circa

Two thousand sixteen: the bridge, the skyline

Lacerated by the outdated skyscrapers;

Somewhere in the wallyards

                                  of the neighborhoods,

Teenagers playing baseball,

The hoop in rusty chains

Swinging

Trembles from a lucky throw.

Photographer

A robot photographer

Wears a cap,

A robot photographer

Calls herself Cap.

She went into the craters of volcanos

And portrayed fishes in the deep blue sea,

But also

Pictures white cups of coffee,

Whenever she encounters one.

"This lens is so bright and clear,

I bought it

On a vintage market."

"Why would you spend

Your efforts on that

When you have a stronger camera embedded

In your bright green eye?"

"Well,

I like the nostalgic blur and that the images

Are leaning towards magenta

When you use these old photo cameras;

Besides, Canon

Is my totem spirit,

We are connected

By invisible ties,

I do believe

(And do not laugh)

That we are relatives, kindred spirits,

I derive

My genealogy from Canon,

Back in times

When Vikings worked themselves into frenzy

And posted random things on Instagram."

Fashionista

A robot fashionista

Installed a wonderful feature, great

App, and has grown

One hundred hands with five hundred nails

So that she

Could actually use

A part of her collection

Of nail polishes before

Betelgeuse explodes.

Gardener

A robot gardener

Knew no sleep, no repose until

He had trimmed the leaves of grass

Cutting them with a sharp blade

                                        of utmost precision,

Creating the field so even that it was painful

To look at it, and whoever wanted

To acquire the moderate pain in the eyes,

Resembling the feel of glass bits and sand dust,

Was advised by medics,

Sometimes insistently,

To go there and stare;

One session

Sometimes was quite enough.

Robotic Unfinished Haiku

A robot therap-

Ist could not believe his ears.

Robot

A robot robot

Told me, "I don't know

What does distinguish a robot from a human

Being, and if I try

To pass for a robot, I always

Have a hard time."

"But you are

Already a robot, you don't have to

Try to pass for a robot, just be yourself."

I offered a well-meaning

But useless piece of advice.

"That's not that simple,"

Snapped the robot robot.

Wizard

an aficionado of

charming anachronisms

of different mechanics:

clocks ticking, running sand,

and artificial flowers

he showed me his collection:

a grand orifice

of the orchid gaped in space,

a hole, an aperture unperturbed,

a dissipating spectrum,

a moistened eye that blinks,

and a wax effigy

of the Eiffel Tower—a miniature,

but in observed proportion

and careful detail.

it seemed that I could walk

along the trail of light

around the Orchid Tower,

and, entertained, arrive

to the place where gentle flowers

blankly refuse to wither.

o sweet anachronisms

of mechanoid wizard.

Pet

If I had a pet,

It would be a coffee machine.

I'd put a collar on it,

Emblazoned with sapphires

And emeralds; I'd take

It on a long walk

Early on a quite chilly

Morning. No, I wouldn't.

It would be a grown-up

Coffee machine, and it

Could have a walk on its

Own.

Robotic Kiss

Let me bestow my kiss

On your forehead ablaze,

Over the great dis-

Tance, by way of pressing

The button in form of heart.

Previous Model

I fell in love with the previous version

Of this robot; do not try to sell me

The new model. I

Am remarkably old-fashioned

And pride myself on it; the old vacuum cleaner,

Which belonged to my grandma,

Is still my faithful pet.

Fury

She flung the door open,

And with contempt,

Throwing a bunch of papers in my face,

                          exclaimed in mad fury:

"Here! This is my manual,

Read it, you... you..."

She grasped for words,

A gazillion lamps flashed in her faceted eyes,

And I

Thought in horror: this must be what

A short circuit looks like.

Decree

a robot sovereign

produced a decree:

it would not

be morally right

to torture humans.

yes, it is true

that humans feel pain sometimes,

but only robots

should be tortured

because their pain

exceeds the pain of humans

by dozens and dozens of megahurts.

what does your theology

and your eschatological sense

tell you?

Important Reminder Haiku

if you discover animal abuse in the household,

please also call

the robot abuse prevention center.

Necromancer

Necromancer

the blatant full moon

outside my window,

and a necromancer

in a white cravat,

her hands in blood,

tries to revive Baudelaire.

Specter

What brought you here,

I have no way of knowing.

A gilded bird led you through the woods,

And in the abandoned hall with broken windows

And broken mirrors,

You found yourself not

Entirely

For no reason, I could tell.

You spoke to me,

And I was moved and shaken,

But counting myself not

Among the living,

I could not help you,

Nor could I assist you,

And neither could I fully sympathize

With your unfortunate self-gratifying

                              involvement

With one of the dim specters of the place.

Ventriloquist

an exorcist a narcissist

in a black cape

enamored necromancer

the wrecked warlock

overly dramatic

thaumaturgist

taxidermist of words

(they stare with red glass eyes

of squirrels and wild pigs;

their dusty fur is broken once you touch it)

ventriloquist of outstanding powers,

making walls eloquently speak and jewel boxes

treasure chests burst

open.

Ouija

Ouija autocorrect

In a dark

Box of a room

Glib cantankerous

Spirits

Quibbling over

Trivial matters

A collection of quick rejoinders

Don't flinch

Stand still

Freeze like that

Do not touch

The vainglorious apple

Lest I miss

On your sweet terrible head

Emperor

Morning

My morning

Starts with a despaired recollection

Of my unfortunate falling out

Of favor of the Emperor.

Procession

When the Emperor

Enters the capital,

Three thousand blue butterflies

Are released in his face;

The petals of pink roses,

The river of wheat

Is thrown under his feet,

Ten thousand green mirrors

Blink in amazement,

As he follows, lowering his head,

Under five hundred triumphal arcs

      adorned with his

    bas-reliefs,

In between two rows of fifty eight marble statues

Depicting him

In childhood,

As a young man,

Now leaning against the wall,

Now reading the letter,

Ordering to kill the captive,

Pardoning the prisoner.

He stops for a moment

In front of one of his marble doppelgängers

And realizes in a split second

That he is mortally wounded.

Motel

The Emperor, eyes shining,

Forgets the approaching enemies

Hunting

Along the sunny road,

Near an abandoned motel,

Drab-winged

Barbushkus Mabitabibus,

A rare specimen.

Escape

Let's grant the herald, the fastest rider,
With precious memories,
                      as many as he could harbor.
Let's good-humorously congratulate each other
That in his scroll there was nothing:
Nothing imperative from the Emperor,
Nothing important, oh, nothing exigent.

He deserves the new boots for his good ride,
If not a golden ring, if not a grey horse.
Forget that in the evil old times
He could have been hanged
                      under the rainy low sky
On an ugly tree with a creaking thread,
Attentively checked and well-twisted.

Approval

A bewildered Emperor

Stands in front of the cage with a dragon,

And decides to implement rigorous restrictions,

Exterminate from now on all the loopholes

                                  in the laws,

For which partly the Party

Was responsible, and partly

The predecessor.

Clearly, dragons should be forbidden

                                  from now on.

On the contrary, all the beautiful creatures,

                                  such as: unicorns,

Porcupines, domestic fishes and animals,

Including but not limited to

Flamingoes, and those who wear

                                  golden leashes with medals,

Not to mention

The chirruping circle of monkeys,

                      scarabs and grackles,

Also

Pride of chameleons,

            one comelier than the other,

Who are gathered on a shining golden plate,

And alike, that is to say, things like that

Meaning innocuous,

        nice in their habits, pleasant to the eye,

As well as having diagonal stripes

Or adamantine gaze

Or both

Are mercifully now, wholeheartedly approved.

Wind

Don't interfere,

O wind,

With a sweet sorrow

Of the Emperor

Missionary

Saint

An empty hall with a ceiling so high

That there is no ceiling,

On the marble plates of the floor

Claws clatter behind columns.

I am pretty sure this is a big dog,

Probably mastiff: strong legs,

Silvery fleece;

It has a collar with copper medals.

Maybe it's a lion.

In a high armchair at the table

A future saint with a tonsure sits,

His fingers flutter above the keyboard.

To his left, a quill is lying,

And blue ink sits in a cubic inkwell.

On a wooden bench his hooded cloak is hanging.

It's chilly outside during this time of the year,

Which is breathing

                with belated snow and sorrow.

Behind his shoulder,

There is a window in which the sky is cloudy,

Geometrically narrowed down

                              to an irregular shape,

Sharp angles;

Advertisement flickers:

A cheerful full-cheeked girl holding

Mugs of foaming beer.

Cars slip out of sight one by one,

And disappear as if grinded by a notched wheel.

The entrance

To the Novoslobodskaya metro station is visible,

Tourists

With diligent photo cameras

                              shoot its adornments,

Glass-stained ornaments which look exactly like

Glass-stained windows of the Church

                of the Holy Panda in New Braunfels.

When the train comes,

The saint has closed his laptop.

With a whistle he calls his pet,

Which emerges in between the columns,

I stop

At the sight of its bloody muzzle;

They are ready

To go.

Sister Disaster

Sister Disaster

With a holy father

Gets into a train.

They're in civil dresses

With silly feathers

On their hats, which are very plain.

Sister Disaster

With the holy father

Orders some tea.

"Do not we make, dear

Father, rather

A good team?"

He throws a glance

At a round window

And squeezes a gun.

Sister Disaster

And the holy father

Are ready to have some fun.

Duck-like Birds

a tonsured monk

composing Latin verse

distributed the caesurae

between the metric feet of equal length,

preserving equilibrium,

while the red-tufted duck-like birds

were diving in the lake

                         just outside high window;

everything fit the meter so perfectly well.

Traveler

A traveler arrives on the wild shore

Where he is met by aboriginal people.

He is tired, a white collar of his shirt

Is grey from his sweat and hardships.

Some obedient natives now take his luggage

And off they go to construct a tent.

The roof will be covered with palm leaves,

And a dinner served of mackerel

                          and boiled tortoise eggs.

The traveler, having changed his shirt

                          for a modest black suit

(Not very formal,

On account of jungles around

And virtual nakedness of the aboriginals)

Follows his guide (whom he calls *cicerone*,

And, later in his ethnographic works

                and memoir, Vergilius)

To the big man of the place

Who is sitting in a high chair,

His elbows resting on polished skulls.

The king takes a pipe out of his long yellow teeth,

And begins his slow tale about the history,

Religion, habits and manners

                of sons of that soil,

Freedom-loving descendants of mighty deities.

The traveler arrived with a mission

To bestow on these good-natured

                but ignorant people

The privileges of literacy and the true belief

                in our Lord almighty.

When the traveler

Sails away, stores of ivory and ebony

                           are onboard,

As well as a treasure chest

            and a wooden statue

                         of a local demon,

He makes sure he has scrupulously scribbled

A recipe for that mackerel.

He is standing on the deck, eyes full

With the bluest mist of the disappearing island.

The traveler thinks about his wife Theresa

And colorful ships of loud Liverpool.

Breakthrough

The incumbent Mater

Iolanthe the Second,

Bishopess of Rome

And the leader of the Catholic Church

Had smoked some pot

Before her speech

On Trafalgar square

That she gave

Advocating the rights of plants.

Succulent among those present

Applauded wildly;

And a passing bird

Left a dropping of gratitude

On a sleeve of Her Holiness' white-golden gown.

Poems in a Male Voice

Straw

Sleep is excess

I was adamant

I insisted

I also noted that she ate too fast

The city was in a blue mist, twisted,

In dusk and dust

"Must I

Drink a cocktail through a straw?"

                                          She asked.

You must drink anything no more;

And in the world her long transparent straw

And scarlet strawberry distinctly coexisted.

Tigers

What is this fascination, I asked,

              with robots,

       lilies,

Grasses, and tigers?

Nothing, really,

She whispered.

It all is not about tigers or lilies,

Neither it is about robots or grasses.

Incomplete Haiku (25), the First Incomplete Haiku in a Male Voice

I wanted you like only

A man accomplished,

Having left nothing to wish,

With a satisfied thirst, could.

Parakeet

Cabaret Voltaire,

Ballet mécanique,

A doll scattering her cogged wheels

While dancing, bowing, and glancing;

                                             a yellow parakeet

Spreads wings

In a glittering ring

Wait, I'll show you something

That you have not seen.

Emerald

Doll, doll, how come I cannot break you

If I want to smash and wreck you,

If I want to disassemble myself

        at the sight of

    emerald

Pouring down cliffs of your lungs,

Dropping on the floor as mercury and requiem;

Freeze like you are for a split second,

Let me reverently commit you to my memory.

Tea

I asked her, Madame,

Would you like some tea,

And while she

Monocled me piercingly,

All cold and with a disdainful smile,

Hated a witness—

A mechanoid snail

Looking out of her embroidered purse,

But I could see

She never once

Would tell me "no,"

And so I stood,

Without a flinch,

By way of small revenge

Returning carefully

No more than a quarter

Of her monstrous smile.

High Heels

I asked her do you like my new high heels,

Does not the calf muscle

Look tighter now, and the calf bone,

Longer? She responded, yes,

It does, it does, but why did you pick up the

Red color, fluorescent in the dusk,

When the black

Is so much better?

And I literally let her

Ask

To dispel and dissipate,

Even though I was aghast,

And I let her

Administer a slow deliberate kiss

Leaving a long-playing aftertaste,

On my poor unlucky mouth.

Beetles

I can hardly stand it,

I ask her what

Time is it, where is the time, who made it

Crumple, why should there be a time,

                              time's defeated,

And is there something in between no-time-ness

                              and timelessness,

And all I hear is "yes" or "no,"

Answered flatly,

Or worse, endless talking

About her collection of rare beetles

With peridot wings and bifurcating antlers,

Magnificent deer antlers and fading whispers;

                              a taxidermist

Made an effigy

Out of one, in adornment

Of the hall of her house.

Corset

She classified things: here is

Pistachio flavor, here is salted

Caramel; gelato and

Ice cream are not to be confused,

Fellatio fallacy is once again disproved;

Whatever needed a distinction, had it,

And I, and I with my abundant sets of thing

That could not bend and fit, and twist out wildly

Of measure and control,

Was put in a tight form, was laced in corset,

Was given an exoskeleton, a case, container,

Like an exhibit in sandglass museum,

Where every sand glass is an hourglass,

But each is turned a second after another,

Because there is but one curator.

Gyroscope

No, you will be not spared,

Once in a lifetime, the light is turned on

And pitilessly cuts objects out of darkness,

A merciless cold light, which leaves

                          no shadow to hide,

Leaves nothing to the sight

                    which wants to be deceived,

The gyroscope rotates, the goal is resistance

To rotation, balance, power, control.

I studied demiurgy, physics, and choreography

                                of words;

And for a pet I kept

A venomous spider, and for a monocle, Venus,

I turned into tiger lilies, lilied tigers,

Swaying-hips lynxes, unleashing gory orgy;

I am myself a gyrator,

And I am forgetting the word.

Wrestling

endless wrestling

is exhausting,

she said and sighed,

and threw her fan on a table.

porcelain tinkled,

a dragon tail

of her red dress

in golden wasps,

twisted around a chair leg;

blue kakadu

in an avocado tree

and a mechanical cicada

mixed a fantastic noise.

I leaned to her

and whispered, yes,

especially when

you do not

want to win

Hair

should she swoosh those doves,

she should know

better,

should the curtain be swished, should I

wish it was closed, if open,

or, if closed, open,

or, if open, open?

either way, by Jove,

either way,

in her hair

of gory rust

in those days of yore, I trust,

I could have her vigor and passion.

I am bound to sense ashes,

apple scent, mold, and dust,

in a sense, to be buried,

I suspect that I must.

Cocoa

Madame, enjoy

Your temporary stay

In our glorious and hospitable state,

And if you ever want to hesitate,

Don't hesitate to hesitate, but do

Hesitate for cooling hot cocoa.

I'd very much like to watch you agonizing

Over chocolate, the greatest accolade

That chocolate deserves, which is

Meticulously agonized over.

Doubt

but if she

did answer me, if she

did,

what

would I do, what I have not undone?

indeed, I would not do much,

nor good indeed.

Look

She looked down on me, which was

Quite a difficult trick, rest assured,

Considering that she sat and I stood.

She looked and issued through her teeth:

"Is this understood?"

I looked at her and could not hold a smile.

I nodded, "Yes. Thoroughly."— "Fine."

Plums

If it was a disgrace

To love you, I—what do you expect?—

Would love you still.

In a plum tree orchard,

Your white dress, in danger of being stained,

Shines, but traces

Of plums are never washed away.

They are never

Washed away, which

Does not mean that they never vanish,

For—

A strange nature of plums—they do

Vanish, they will fade away,

All by themselves,

Unless you replenish

The stores of your stains

By walking with me again

In a plum orchard.

Oh, I would love you still, in a net of shadows

That breach the unity of your celestial body,

Break you into

A multitudinous agglomeration

                              of quick fragments,

And liquefy your hair as well as your eyes,

Full of mercurial instability and radiance.

And were you to ask again,

I'd answer, I would love you still,

Even if it was silly (which it is not),

Or, what is worse,

To be expected.

Belligerent Venus

No, never mind,

No one

Is made of sand,

No one of marble,

And out of salt.

No river could be set

On fire; I

Would not kill an ant,

Not even a fire ant.

Via a spiral staircase,

Orpheus ascended to Hades

To cast a last reproachful glance at Eurydice.

A cactus in an antique ceramic pot

Proliferates under the warm sun

And blooms purple, its tentacles waving into

A strange sculpture, which, in semi-dark,

Reminds me of Venus; all reminds me of Venus,

Except for Venus,

Which reminds me of Mars.

Zipper

Let your slender hand, with a jingling bracelet,

Travel across the blanket to meet a zipper,

Which would not yield at first,

                                        I would jinx zippers,

Slide faster, faster

A snake of a hand.

If I am

Allowed to issue

A modest and polite,

Most unassuming,

Request,

I'd ask you to please

                      undo this knot in your throat; it

Is nearly asphyxiating you,

But let your jingling, mesmerizing bracelet on.

Adele

The landscape of her shoulders

Was so wide, so

Convoluted, I

Found myself

Completely lost.

Adele, if that's your name,

Adele, how can you bear

To look at your shoulders

Every foggy morning

In the mirror, stained

With fingerprints and your glimpses,

Blotches of toothpaste,

Where your reflection lingers?

Languid smiles

Blink as red and yellow fish

In a dark pond,

And every evening, as the chandeliers

Drop golden tears

On scarlet, velvet drapes,

If that's your name, Adele?

Vanilla

She was gleaming

With a fervor close to

Religious

As she asked if I would prefer

Pistachio (I would) to

Vanilla, or

Vice versa.

Vermont,

Pierrot,

I could not

Care,

Any.

I swear I'll make you recite into my ear

Your insufferable, unendurable lines.

Artist

you watched,

appearing calm, if not cold,

contemplating

new dimensions

of pain and pleasure,

as I was

portraying you in all the glory

                                    and agony

of your dream anatomy, without

omitting as much as

the slightest detail,

a drop of sweat,

a fold of ecstasy, a fragment,

I,

the frantically lucky artist.

Hypnotizer

I swung a golden watch on a thin chain,

enjoying its faint swish,

in front of your green-honey eyes,

and you enjoyed it;

tell me,

didn't you?

Nest

Unknown terrors weaved a nest

In her sad soul, laid eggs to hatch

And produce offspring, crying

In desperation of hunger and out of will

To live,

Licking their sleek tails,

Demanding wriggling worms,

                                   and so their parents

Fed them, beak to beak, and I could see

Every quiver in her transparent eyes,

                                   my hair standing

On end, while she was breaking her mouth

Into a very quiet, calm smile.

Tweezers

She squeezed

Tweezers, see?

What is she

To do with them,

Zeus merciful?

Butterfly

She sat down across the table from me and said,

I could not hear what, but I saw

In perfect

Suspension,

Her artificial red lips, moving

As though on a slow-motion video. A light arm.

It was so, I do not know,

Horrific, or

I was intimidated, as though

She was about to catch a butterfly,

Awkwardly flapping in the air,

With this impossible red mouth of hers.

And, to be sure, the butterfly appeared,

Lazuli wings and orange flashes and antlers,

Thrown into

Trepidation, trembling, and blinking,

                                            bright-blue ashes,

Fluttering near the terrifying trap.

Galatea

—but darling, you practically made

me; I'm your Galatea, metanoia, aren't I, please?

—you'll find salt on the counter in an amoretto

                              porcelain figurine.

calm down a bit, and gulp a chalice of tears.

Humbly Asking

I started talking with no intent

to suffocate you,

that's where we are:

you, in the stripes of a sun-beamed, inflated tent,

and I,

could I disjoint limb from graceful limb,

hands from your torso, unscrew your legs,

and gently detach

the paragon of the curved shape

from what, I'm certain, rightfully appears

to be your lips,

separate this from that?

no?

why

not?

ah, I was imploring, I was begging you.

Green Shoes

she stopped in front of me in her green shoes

and slowly said:

"if I were courageous, if

I were heroic,

I'd tell you an absolute *yes*.

In that I'd be very

true to myself.

I would have plunged into it, if

I were lionhearted."

that was the sweetest,

the weakest "no" in existence,

which I was going

to brush aside.

Gloves

Your attire

Looks different from what

You usually wear,

I cannot decide if it is

This ridiculous pompous feather

Or the impression of vague absence, which

Missing gloves produce;

Their absence is no doubt

                              a pretext for something,

A hidden message, a hint,

But as I imagine that green skin,

Wrinkled around your wrist,

On which a bracelet dangles,

I feel a light anxiety, a tremble,

And could not help but wonder,

As though not only

They were lost

But that it was I who lost them.

Imploring

Once again forgive me. I
Do not dare to ask about
Anything but do forgive
Without notice, as a cloud
Forgoes its form, without
Thought, intention, or desire.
Once again I am sorry. I
Am rude and I am cruel,
And I absolutely could not
Be any ruder or any crueler.

Form

he forlornly

and sternly

informed her

of the sterility of form:

the form

is calamitous,

firm, fragile,

the stalactite

of limestone

is ruinous

and is about to

crash down,

and if he could, he would not have

much of a form himself, himself

adagio.

Alchemist

Automaton

as a monstrous full-blown moon

transmogrified itself slowly into the face of

my pale automaton, who hides her beauty by veil

of clouds and imperturbability of marble,

I looked

in endless grief, in devastating sorrow,

at both the moon and her thin, pallid features.

ah maybe for the sake of love and dolor

I should not breathe in life in such finesse,

but leave her cold, untouched, unspoiled,

                                                undamaged,

never pour in her ears the sweet viscous poison

of my long-dispelling words, never

try to envenom her marble existence

                                    with my longing, never

make her shudder in a spasm of pain

                                    and excitement, never

make her alive.

Table

here is the Pandora's box, opened,

here the Perseus's shield, I apply my lipstick

                          looking in it;

that, with a stamp of a lion rampant

            and a golden eagle whose body

is covered with many blue eyes vigilant,

                          wide-open,

is an envelope with the full list of all

                      the living beings,

and a request from the trembling demon

            of the third circle of inferno

to serve me humbly,

in the bloody muzzle

to bring me my slippers in the morning

and kiss fingers,

here

is a retort with an emerald bliss,

the elixir of life and panacea

for all maladies;

the alkahest which I, of course, invented

dissolved the bottle and left a round trace,

and the philosopher's stone serves

                              as a *presse-papier*.

Formula

as I was pouring, in my concentration,
a cup of mercury into a bowl of liquid silver,

I suddenly remembered, rediscovered
that awesome, easy formula, with which

the pale automaton should be enlivened
and breathe on her own,

                to look into the ruined mirrors,

see mercury and silver in her eyes, laugh, play,
be angry, write rejections, invitations,

drink tea with me in a garden abuzz with bees
                            and bugs,
pick a favorite flower
          among the abundance of flowers,

construct a paper bird and paper frog

and make them

                leap from the table with her exhale.

Mandragora

mandragora root, elongating on your eyes,
    with a mouth of harlequin smiling awry
        cutting out of its small face,
a pity,
I think that I forgot a crucial ingredient
                        and it will never
start speaking

Heart

boiling blood

in the clepsydra

reappearing

on the exoskeleton

of armor, I could see a scarlet stain

ever-widening where I expected

to discover

my hard heart, intact and tacit

and I saw it, and I saw it

but consenting to be broken

Plan

distracted

scattered

counting leaves

and interrupting the count

time and again

I have that mold

into which I'm going to squeeze it

that thing of strange configuration

that disassembled

that dissected thing

cut out of one's chest

or put in a jar

with spirit

in between three-

dimensional models

of peculiar grasses

and Democritus atoms of great size

to preserve

for future generations

excursionists

a curiosity of sorts

a rarity I'd say

oh it would adorn

the laboratory.

where?

between

a two-headed rabbit

and a calf with a beak

Distillatio

Again I wake up

With a cube of your name in my mouth,

And must

Decide,

Drop it on the pillow or swallow

Before

The first inhale,

And a happy one, too; triumphant

Over the failure, faltering, and fleeting,

I could not care if I can't use the word "love"

For a number of reasons, because what is it then,

If I want

To ask you to hold me a bit tighter,

To let me feed on your exploring mouth,

Dissecting hands, to beg you

To be true to your words, transmute them,

                                distill a diamond

In a triangle retort

Out of fine fantasy, out of

Multiple realities, conflicting,

                               but falling into concord,

To resurrect your love, but

Am I really that cruel?

Book

> *All summer I emptied myself and contemplated*
> *Love, transition...*
>
> Cyril Hurk

All summer I emptied myself, persistently
Freeing myself from the clutches
                     of helpless demons.
All summer I've been annoyed and vexed,
                             complaining
To shaking trees and paradisaic flowers shaking,
And training lackadaisical dark shadows
To obey me
Many a shadow as thick as strawberry jam
                     spread across a loaf of bread;
And in the third leaf of the three-fold mirror
                            my reflection
Did not always show up all summer.
All summer evenings, a bee loud like a drummer

Excited me and hovered above

                              the unprotected skin

And threatened to assault

And numb me.

All summer I was busy, filled a crystal-clear jar

                              with pink petals

Running to the ground from

                              the clepsydrae of shrubs,

I learned from an old book that one drop of blood

                            of the antlered frog

          will splendidly suffice,

Commingled with leaches' blue blood,

                            to make a desired effect,

But opted for my own cataleptic

Throbs,

And spared you,

Leaving you neither undead, nor dead.

Golem's Revolt

Didn't I feed you with my nipples

On a bitter milk of woe,

On the gore of monstrous joy

And elated

Remembering of death

                    triumphantly approaching?

Red terrors of grass twisted

                between our light legs in sandals.

I wanted

To bring you to the verge of living

Out of bleakness of your nonexistence;

I filled in with my endless power

Your emptiness; it did not

Overwhelm me.

I exhaled into your mouth words

                        evoking trembling specters,

I summoned worlds and populated devastated,

                              dreary landscapes

With dogheaded gods and robots,

Beasts with sharp wings,

Tender peacocks.

You were clad in a golden tunic,

I gave you a rose-quarts rosary beads,

The iron stick with a handle

                        of the basilisk's yellow eye

With a vertical ink pupil.

Trepidation

Crowned your head,

And you, the golem, the sweet dust,

                            the lump of clay,

And you want to overrule me?

Chess

If I had to do anything but chew

Marmalade, I think my profession would be,

To scale chess figures, red against white, white

Against black, nigredo,

Rubedo, citrinitas, albedo.

It is important to the game of chess

That the figures are of the very same range,

                shape, and weight, and color.

So, I'd dedicate myself entirely to that,

And wear an apron, and get the sharpest lens

Installed into my eye.

And morning to dusk, I would weigh ideal pieces,

                without cessation,

Until I reached a perfect

Equilibrium, an unperturbed equation.

Command

Henceforth,

I

Command you:

Stop being solid,

Flower, and pour

Your fragrant

Essence down

The narrow throat

Of an amber-yellow bottle.

Could you be

A smoke or liquid

Essence of bliss,

If not forgetting, then

Forgetfulness, at least?

Of course, you could—

I told you, be.

Beast

but

yes,

it is a feast,

as a golden-collared,

paper-leashed swift beast

licks milk out of a silver ringing bowl.

I am prone

to repetition of a drowsy monotone,

a monologue that enters an open door,

swishes to an open window,

and permeates me to the bone.

in a gravure where beasts commingled

with plants, angels with

you-remember-who, machines with deities,

and goddesses with whores,

I spotted the flickering smile

of a snow leopard,

a symbol of snow,

an allegory of parliament,

and knew immediately how to summon snow.

Stranger

Ribs of the sky, exposed;

Grass, heavy with seeds, leans

To the ground. The planet spins around

Its gossamer axis,

Flipping past the equinox and solstice,

Never stopping, throwing grass

In thrusts, and making

Leaves heavy;

Stems—drying, leaning, breaking—

Under the unbearable fruits' burden.

A masked, bird-beaked stranger,

Under cover, with

Her bare-boned smiling face, exposed teeth,

Gathers midnight seeds in dusty pockets,

Where she keeps

A monocle with scratched rainbow glass,

A feather, a broken model toy car,

A watch with a lid,

And a tiny bottle

Of salt.

Sprinkled with a wonderful solution,

Preventing vertigo at times of circumvolution,

The salt fantastic could depress and could exalt.

Golem

You lie, a pile of clay;

Were I to write

Ash letters

On your forehead,

Your chest would expand,

Containing a clay

Heated heart,

And lungs would unfold,

Alveoli opening one by one,

And air would hiss, exiting

Through your brown teeth,

And you would rise,

Open your lashless eyes,

And smile at me

With a terrifying smile

Of loyalty conflated

With suspicion.

But if you grew

Too strong,

I would erase

The first letter

From your forehead,

And instantaneously,

You would fall dead,

And on a pile of clay,

Amorphous,

Blue,

Your phallus

Curling

Like a helpless snake.

Fine Dust

Another day spent turning hard pages

Of incunabula in vain attempts

                              to tame a succubus,

Day spent gulping spoonfuls of

Fine dust

Instead of demanding your kisses,

Dimming light,

In shadows of lenient, drooping succulents.

My fair share of days aired

                              with impossible grandeur,

Of lack, regret, and sweet anguish,

Aerated blood,

Flashing agonies,

Like dashing silver and scarlet fish,

Days full of stops upon entrance, displaced

Egresses, a want I never unleashed,

Save several spirits of lilied light-pawed tigresses,

Escaping and dispersing in silence and amidst

Silences.

Transmutation

A moon rolling in zenith

And ringing there

Like an annoying bell,

A ripe fruit, about to burst with seeds,

Fails to distract

A thaumaturgist busy with

Distilling:

Tears drop in a retort

And evaporate, a rainbow glass

Reflects fire and mist in a scrying sphere

On a jade tripod,

The green blood of a squashed toad

Is running up a lucid spiral cord,

And if I succeed, I would boil it down to

A smooth, glimmering stone

Of unalloyed love, transmuted

Out of pure, asphyxiating wrath.

Calligrapher

Made a living being a subject of an amazing art:

Stereoscopic eyes, styrofoam body, and

Covered with alabaster dust, face,

Asking a question gently,

And waiting for an answer; what kind of answer

Do I expect?

Bend a soul

Into a 'D' of a clandestine

Calligraphy:

As soon as the two dots, known as colon,

Precede the 'D' into a certain

Magical terrain, a great realm,

          a space of the alchemic permutations,

The letter turns into laughter itself,

                        emitted neither

By you—and on my temple

          I could sense your breath—

Nor by me.

If I was to—

Calligraphically—draw

Your name, I'd invest some effort into it,

But never did I have

Persistency which is required for such art;

Were I not lazy, I would extract golden ink from

My vein's inkwell,

And blue-laguna lapis lazuli

Out of my eyes,

And I would draw your psychedelic name

On the most even, smoothest paper I could find.

Instead I create worlds: one between

Your each inhale and exhale,

                       and watch them grow, rainbow

Bubbles bursting in the air—see this one to reel—

If only to besprinkle

    my contracted pupils with sparkling shards.

But what of it. I could not mind some tears.

Summoning a Demon

You were entitled

To become my darling, darling,

You

Accepted it so gracefully, as a

Predicament which is greater

Than you,

A duty

From which there was no sure way to escape

But you would rather

Evade it if you could, still,

You did accept—

The unavoidable void,

A video game, made to

Denote

And designate the outside world,

Define and

Multiply

Perform the operations

Of distillation, dissolution,

Permutation,

Magnetization, condensation,

Heating, freezing,

Evaporation, vertigo, and sublimation—

All usual alchemical routine.

And, tracing with your black blood

                         the ornament on the carpet,

I have to thank you;

               you've been a wonderful target.

Dispute

How many angels may be positioned on
The point of a needle,
And how many demons fit in a thimble,
Is a scholarly discussion
To be had
In a library hall
         with mirrors and dark bookshelves,
Marble statues
    arguing silently by way of daring glares,
Unmoved duels.

Keep your mantle away
        from their mischievous sandals;
One of the statues is known
        to jump on the tails of
Respected academics, to everyone's amusement.

"And so, you purport, my dear sir, that angels
Could be situated

On a needle's point in multiple quantities.

However,

Here

I shall prove to you that you are mistaken,

Only one angel gets it,"

She said and with a visible effort

Inserted a long rusty needle

Into his chest.

He smiled with bloodless lips

                        and bowed slightly, uttering:

"This is not something I could disavow."

Statues whispered into each other's marble ears

Faltering words of stupefied surprise.

Letters

Death in a scarlet cloak

Led my pen with its fragile fingers;

                      my pen flew above the page,

And a skeletal hand held a lamp, the dim

Dusk did not disperse at the weak ray,

As I was straining my eyes to obtain a vision

Of things above the wall; I saw a city

Which belonged to the future,

But death's foul breath

On the back of my neck

Was like a surge of the cold air;

The brass scales

And mason jars

With homunculi, concoctions,

                      alloys, and poisons

Glistened, covered with dust,

In the extinguishing light and faded out,

But my letters

Kept glimmering.

Spirit

I summoned a spirit; care to see? Here

It is. In unremitting rain,

It is disturbed and purples on the edges;

In shine, it is upset and cries bitterly;

And, in full moon, relentlessly, it glides

Between the shelves, the table, the piano;

In shooting starshowers,

Ever more translucent,

It freezes, with its breath, my chandeliers

And pierces, with its sword,

                              unharmed marble nymphs,

Or walks through walls,

Indiffcrent, inattentive,

I'd even say as much as scatterbrained,

But it collects its brain in a silver helmet.

Paper Flowers

Chamomile

Ah chamomile, paper flower,

                                      why are you so sad, is it

Because your petals fall into water

And run aground? Your tears...

At a sudden gush of wind you fall apart

Don't disappear just yet

But may I ask

Please disregard your plight,

Your faithfulness to your predicament,

Love to your fate, *amor*

Fati, fatigue, a solemn pledge?

You pledged allegiance to decay and mold,

To mildewed surfaces and rusticating rust,

Sand, yellow grass, glass slowly

                                        moving on your eyes,

Like the reluctant liquid,

                                        dilapidated mirrors, cast

As shadows, with ruined mercury ground; must

I list more?—soot, charcoal glitter, star dust.

Iris and Hibiscus

An iris with the head of an ibis,

Among the irises, grew fatter

In the greasy soil; nearby, a hibiscus

Grew, with the head of a dreary sparrow,

In red soil, dry and salty.

Iris

very well, but how could *the iris* be a flower

              if I knew for so long,

      Osiris dear,

that it's a bird with a red beak

              and a blue eye that pierces night,

and when I walk around the flower-

bed, I try to watch my hem and slippers,

lest irisi would bite,

I know them, they're all creepers

all, I tell you not

forget

I jest you not,

dismiss me not

they look at me, and all I ask is

please don't stare me dead

Daffodil

a daffodil is a treasure of my sight,

a folly of Lilith materialized, *narcissus*

pseudonarcissicus (as I read in a thick book,

abbreviated for the usages of man),

a daffodil is a one-hundred-dimensional piece

(I spared myself, I would not have to be pleased)

a silly daffodil, a haughty fragment of space,

watch as you run aground and converse

there

into something else

Hyacinth and Fleur-De-Lis

Who would you choose

between glistening hyacinth

and flexible fleur-de-lis?

Truth be told,

I would trade both

for a rose.

Liar, you won't trade both.

Maybe I won't. Maybe I would trade both.

Dandelion

a wind blows and ruins a flower, wet

                      petal drip

            drop

         drip

I wish I could grasp your tiny umbrella,

your parachute, your weak limb

and fly into some viscous space in between

two rows of clouds,

a sad mime, mimetic artist,

                        numismatist of tin cans,

a numerologist of letters,

                        and a writer of long pauses

I wish I was as vain as

a dandelion

undoubtedly is,

a dandy, a lion

        smiling, at ease

with its predicament to rip my heart apart

and you watch as I construct

it

dot by dot

don't

do it

don't

Orchid

Origami of orchid

Unfolds and I am staring at sharp edges,

With your hard name in my red mouth,

Aquiver, fledged

Arrow, a sharp syllable ripping my lips,

A breaking split, depleting and escaping,

A small narrow pointed missile, blinding dart,

A dirty word, an expletive, a curse,

And thrown ashore, to run dry and expire,

I'll still succeed to set your mind afire

And heart racing.

Rose

The reddest rose

I found, adored, and smelled.

I told the rose she will be mine,

And she replied, she shan't.

Ah, very well. Then stay

Just where you are.

And she said, nah.

What do you want?

And she replied, your heart.

Why do you need my heart for?

It is hard

And

Heavy;

With the reddest

Rose's sharpest spear,

The bluest rapier,

My heart is pierced through,

My poor heart is pierced.

Muzzle

This muzzle

looks like a rose

and then again like a muzzle

which it is.

Flower

I stole your name

And wear it

As I would wear a flower

If I were wearing flowers.

Were it a flower,

I would be wearing flowers.

Unknown Flower

I traversed the fields stained

With red, blue, yellow, and white,

Mottled fields brimming with flowers,

When I came across

A flower

Unusual

A flower

Rather weird

Resembling a bird in fact

Standing on one leg

Of its exceptionally long, thin, and strong stem.

It reminded me of you.

Of your short curly hair

And protruding out of its glorious

                            chestnut-color mass

That thin, sharp nose of yours.

And I gazed at the flower

For quite a while,

It grew shieldless, and I could see of course

That it was remarkably resilient,

A stubborn flower of the colossal will to live

As well as odd beauty

And I thought whether I want to break its stem

And take it

Or I should leave it untouched,

To grow and to wither

Without hastening its curt life,

Without bringing it immediately

                         to the point of quick dying,

As I wanted.

I hesitated.

I wavered.

It seemed to beg me "break me."

Still, I was reluctant.

Unnaturally Bright Flower

Can't be true, can it?

Look at this thing, called

Phalaenopsis Orchid,

Cannot be better,

It looks at you and shines as though it is a source

Of light. Its name

Explains it.

Disturb Me Not

forget me not,

perturb me not,

disturb me, please,

remember yet,

lest I myself forget.

Forget Me Not

Let forget-me-nots forget me.

Not a flower will be left intact and untwisted

                          during the ceremony

Of renaming flowers and twisting flowers,

                          but let me

Tell you something, when you take

The summer's gossamer from your face,

It will leave a trace across your sharp cheekbones

                                forever.

I will recognize it

Through times and spaces,

Like a scar

      that you could not help but remember.

Purple Dandelion

purple poplar fluff

purple dandelions, flown,

taken by wind, lost, gone,

like the most certain terrestrial realm,

the reign of rain which has evaporated,

like the utopia of the soundest control, a cloud,

and measure, the state of affairs

                                        and lions kissing tigers

in the coat of arms, where everything is ruled,

everything is supervised, surveyed,

and overseen, by a supreme will

and vigilance

of the caesarean and ethereal goner

Mirrors

Reflection

A big fish of her body

Packed in a pink dress,

Carried a certain weight.

She stretched herself along a big mirror,

Leaning to its cold surface,

Kissing her pink reflection.

Mirror

I imagine you

Looking in the mirror

What kind of kingdoms

Do you see there?

What kind of rococo abundance,

Abandoned towers,

A market in Morocco,

Full of fruits, birds, and fabrics,

A restaurant in São Paulo

You are looking in the mirror—

One can imagine—

Seeing there a beast with short golden fur,

A kind of stone sculpture,

A sphinx full of onyx eyes,

And a silk lace of a monocle

Falling down on your mackintosh

On a rainy day,

There is a fish swimming

                          in the depths of your mirror,

It comes closer to the surface

                          in its yellow swimming suit,

And waving its tail

Hides in the blue weeds, only her red eye shining.

On a sunny day,

You probably look at a griffin,

An avid reader of *The New Yorker* on twitter;

He is glancing askance,

Scrolling down the mirror,

And, briefly meeting with you,

Goes on with his morning

                          drinking a cup of *Earl Grey*,

Eating an egg with fried bacon and grape jam.

Lucky you,

I wish I could look in your mirror.

Mirror

Mirror, mirror on the wall,

Tell me how to kill them all.

Mirror

I refuse to be reflected by this mirror,

I have to be reflected elsewhere.

Mirrors

Every time half-expecting

To see something different

For a change

Every time seeing the same things

Conspiracy

Of mirrors

Remarkable persistence

Deserving a better application.

Again I Am Here

again I am here, no corner is in semi-darkness

and only repetitious clicking

of a remote train

like a lucid skeleton of wind dragging itself down

it interrupts itself

with the continuation of the same

reverberating sound

but did I miss this room invaded by mirrors

where ceiling is reflected by the floor?

About the Author

Vasilina Orlova is currently working on her PhD in anthropology from the University of Texas at Austin. She holds a PhD in philosophy from Moscow State University (2013). She has published a number of books of prose and poetry in Russian, including *Mificheskaya Geographia* (*Mythical Geography*, Voimega, Moscow, 2016), *Kvartet* (*Quartet*, Vagrius, Moscow, 2009), *Pustinya* (*The Wilderness*, Zebra E, Moscow, 2008), *Vchera* (*Yesterday*, Greita, Moscow, 2003). Her prose and poetry has appeared in prominent Russian literary journals such as *Noviy Mir*, *Druzhba Narodov*, and *Oktyabr*. She has received several Russian literary awards.

Born in the settlement of Dunay in the Russian Far East in 1979, Orlova has lived in Moscow, London, and is now based in Austin, Texas. She has written in English since 2012. Her first book of poetry in English, *Contemporary Bestiary*, was published in 2014 by Gutenberg Printing Press Independent Group, Austin. Composer Matthew Manchillas wrote a series of songs for soprano, flute, Bb clarinet, and piano, inspired by several poems from *Contemporary Bestiary*, and gave his collection the same title.

Orlova translates both classic and contemporary Russian poets into English—among the classics are Akhmatova, Khlebnikov, and Kharms, and among the contemporaries are Vitaly Pukhanov, Danila Davydov, and German Lukomnikov, as well as anonymous authors of what she calls "urban scribbles" (graffiti). Among poets whose works Orlova has translated into Russian are Dorothy Parker, Mary Barnard, Billy Collins, Margaret Atwood. Orlova's works have been translated into English, French, Spanish, Dutch, Bulgarian, Ukrainian, and Russian. Her writings in English have appeared in different collected volumes and journals, including *The End of Austin*, *Blue Bonnet Review*, *Bloodstone Review*, *Visions International*, and *Cultural Anthropology*.

www.ingramcontent.com/pod-product-compliance
Lightning Source LLC
Chambersburg PA
CBHW022357040426
42450CB00005B/230